MW01173040

I AM THE ONLY ME
Copyright © 2024 by AUDRA SCOTT
ISBN: 979-8-9901529-1-5
Library of Congress Control Number: 2024907806
Published in Austin, Texas

This book is dedicated to...

God Almighty

My nieces and nephews, Patricia Tennison, Jefferson Scott, Ethan Scott, and Kendall Pace-Anderson.

May you always know the uniqueness that lies inside you!

I Am the Only Me

Written by:
Audra Scott

Illustrated by:
Mirabel Lily

The sun gets to make its presence known,

from the hills to valleys and the unknown.

the piano makes gentle tones like the wind that passes through barren lands.

The shadows on the moon get to create different shapes,

that causes us to sit back and observe the beautiful space.

Planes get to soar above the clouds,

to take people where
they want to go
through miles and
miles.

I am the only one who can talk like I can.

Audra Scott is a long time vocalist and educator. She has traveled abroad extensively and has had opportunities she could not have imagined. Her desire is to uplift and encourage performers to dream big, sing loud, and live beyond their wildest dreams.

Audra currently resides in the Dallas/ Fort Worth area.

Made in the USA
Columbia, SC
03 August 2024